21st Century Junior Library

WORKING AT CITY HALL

by Lucia Raatma

CHERRY LAKE PUBLISHING * ANN ARBOR, MICHIGAN

CHERRY
LAKE
Publishing

Published in the United States of America by Cherry Lake Publishing
Ann Arbor, Michigan
www.cherrylakepublishing.com

Content Adviser: Michael Kowski Jr., City Planner, Tinley Park, Illinois

Photo Credits: Cover, ©Yuri_arcurs/Dreamstime.com and ©iStockphoto.com/Juanmonino; cover
and page 6, ©iStockphoto.com/cosmonaut; cover and page 14, ©iStockphoto.com/dlewis33;
page 4, ©iStockphoto.com/lissart; page 8, ©iStockphoto.com/SunChan; pages 10 and 20, ©Jeff
Greenberg/Alamy; page 12, ©iStockphoto.com/nicolesy; page 16, ©iStockphoto.com/Silvrshootr.;
page 18, ©Dmitriy Shironosov/Shutterstock, Inc.

LIBRARY OF CONGRESS CATALOGING-IN-PUBLICATION DATA
Raatma, Lucia.
  Working at city hall/by Lucia Raatma.
    p. cm.—(21st century junior library)
  Includes bibliographical references and index.
  ISBN-13: 978-1-60279-981-3 (lib. bdg.)
  ISBN-10: 1-60279-981-4 (lib. bdg.)
  1. Municipal government—United States—Juvenile literature. 2. City councils—United States—Juvenile
literature. I. Title. II. Series.
  JS346.R33 2011
  352.16023'73—dc22   2010029986

*Cherry Lake Publishing would like to acknowledge the work of
The Partnership for 21st Century Skills.
Please visit www.21stcenturyskills.org for more information.*

Printed in the United States of America
Corporate Graphics Inc.
January 2011
CLSP08

CONTENTS

What do you like to do at the park?

What Is City Hall?

You probably like playing at the local park. You walk on sidewalks to get there. Who takes care of the park and sidewalks? City workers! Many of them work at city hall.

Some city halls are big, old buildings.

City Hall Workers

Many people work at city hall. They make sure your garbage and recycling get picked up. They make sure the **sewer system** is always working. They fix bumpy roads. They help provide important services to everyone in your city.

City council members work as a team to make decisions.

City **council** members talk about **local** problems at meetings. They work on the **budget**. They decide how to spend **taxes**. The city's people vote to **elect** the council members.

The city **recorder** goes to city council meetings. She keeps track of what everyone says at meetings.

Sometimes mayors give speeches about the cities they lead.

The **mayor** also works at city hall. People who live in the city elect him to be the leader of the city **government**. The mayor listens to the people. He wants to make the city better. He goes to special events and meetings. He talks to other leaders about important issues.

Look!

Do you know who your mayor is? Try to look for him in your town. Check the newspaper to see a picture of the mayor. See if he comes to a parade or the opening of a store. How often do you see the mayor in a month?

City managers are busy people.

The city manager keeps track of everything. She makes sure all the city workers are doing their jobs. She also schedules fun events like parades and farmers' markets.

Create!

Go to an event in your town. Maybe it will be a fair or parade. Take photos of people there. Pay attention to the people who are running the event. Then make a scrapbook. Write about the people in your photos.

Tax dollars pay for the things that help keep the city running smoothly.

In every town, people and businesses pay taxes. This money pays for schools, police officers, and other services. A **treasurer** works at city hall. She uses the money from taxes to pay city workers. She also uses it to pay for things the city needs.

Ask Questions! Talk to your parents or other adults about the taxes they pay. Do they think some city projects should get more money? What projects do you think are important?

Your teacher can help you learn more about city government.

Do You Want to Work at City Hall?

There is a lot of action at city hall. Do you want to work there? You can start learning about local government now. At school, you can learn more in social studies.

Maybe one day you will work at city hall!

Ask a teacher if you can take a tour of city hall. Find out which people have offices there. Learn more about your mayor and city council. Your town needs you and your ideas!

Make a Guess!

How many people work at city hall? Go to your city hall Web site and see if you can find out. You might be surprised at how many people work to keep your town running!

GLOSSARY

budget (BUH-jut) a plan for how money will be earned and spent

council (KOUN-suhl) a group of people who help run a town or city

elect (ih-LEKT) choose by voting

government (GUH-vurn-muhnt) a system that uses laws to control a country, state, city, or town

local (LOH-kuhl) describing the area where you live

mayor (MAY-ur) the leader of a town or city government

recorder (rih-KOR-dur) a person who keeps track of events or information

services (SUR-vuss-siz) useful and important things that are provided for people

sewer system (SOO-ur SISS-tuhm) underground pipes that take away rainwater and waste

taxes (TAK-sez) money that people and businesses pay to support a government

treasurer (TRE-zhuh-rur) person in charge of managing money

FIND OUT MORE

BOOKS

Attebury, Nancy Garhan. *Out and About at City Hall*. Minneapolis: Picture Window Books, 2006.

Harris, Nancy. *What's a Mayor?* Chicago: Heinemann Educational Books, 2008.

WEB SITES

Ben's Guide to U.S. Government for Kids

bensguide.gpo.gov/
Explore state and national government topics, all arranged by grade level.

Great Government for Kids

www.cccoe.net/govern/
Learn more about local government with a city hall scavenger hunt. You can also see what a city council meeting is like.

INDEX

ABOUT THE AUTHOR

Lucia Raatma has written dozens of books for young readers. She and her family live in the Tampa Bay area of Florida. Her kids really like playing in the local parks. Thanks, city hall!